ORCHESTRA CONFIDENTIAL

A Survival Guide for Musicians and Those Who Love Them

Mark Gould

Illustrated by
Jeffrey Curnow

Published by Gray Productions
Guttenberg, New Jersey

Acknowledgements

First and foremost a big thank you to Jeff Curnow whose illustrations make the book "sing" in the right key. Jeff encouraged me all the way through the writing process and pushed me to the finish line. Also, a thank you to my patient editors, Judy Corcoran and Wendy Schwartz. They kept me on track and made the more obscure passages more understandable.

Thank you to all the people who previewed various sections of the book and offered good suggestions and encouragement: Annamae Goldstein, Ellen DePasquale, Brian McWhorter, Kevin Cobb, Claudia Arieta, Terry Orr and Alan Colin.

Thank you to my sons, Owen and Sam, who always keep me honest.

And of course, thanks to my colleagues in the many orchestras I've played in and conducted. They have given me an endless supply of source material, without which this book would not have been possible.

TABLE OF CONTENTS

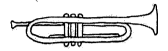

INTRODUCTION

When I began this project about a year ago, it was my intention to write a light-hearted guide for the newly minted members of symphony orchestras—a handbook for orchestra neophytes to inform them about what to expect and what common pitfalls to avoid as they embark upon their orchestral careers. The book is full of advice and "dos and don'ts" for new and hardened veterans alike in the very high-pressure environment of the orchestra.

But after I showed some early drafts of *Orchestra Confidential* to a couple of "civilians" (non-musician music lovers), I saw the book's potential differently. *Orchestra Confidential* has morphed into a handbook/ field guide for the musician, music lover, and anyone really interested in what life in an orchestra is all about.

Orchestra Confidential is not as much a behind-the-scenes-tell-all soap opera about the sordid and debauched lives of classical musicians, like the

Amazon series, *Mozart in the Jungle*. (The book of the same name was a much more accurate depiction of a musician's life but not sexy enough for an Amazon series.) Instead, what's here is a non-technical, decidedly off-kilter description of what is very visible and audible right in front of your face when you attend an orchestra concert.

First, I do a "drunk history" of each section of the orchestra. I discuss the topography and climate of the four fiefdoms: string, woodwind, brass, and percussion. Then I examine the specific nature of each instrument in that fiefdom. This includes material that may seem rudimentary and obvious to musicians, but gives the civilian a clearer perspective on how things operate, musically and personally, inside the orchestra. It's a peek at what goes on inside the brains of the formally dressed people with unsmiling, serious faces on the stage and in the pit: tasty nuggets for the music loving voyeur.

I describe the musical role each instrument plays, with reference to specific repertoire. The repertoire and musical character portrayed by each instrument leads to a discussion of the temperament and personality of the players who choose that particular instrument. For example, why would a person choose to play a bassoon or, in a Zen world-view, why would the bassoon choose them?

Some material technical questions may arise for the uninitiated, such as "reed chirping" or the "bore size" of a bass trombone or the difference between treble and alto clef. If someone is interested to learn more about these technical matters, I would implore you, dear reader, not to look up the information online. Instead, seek out a musician and ask them to explain. This musical outreach may in some small way keep orchestral music alive and thriving. Befriend a musician. Start a conversation with them. We musicians need all the friends we can get these days.

The last part of *Orchestra Confidential* is a meditation on conductors and conducting. This was the most difficult part to the book to write because so much has been written on the subject of conducting, often by conductors themselves. I try to cut through the blather and boilerplate and the avalanche of verbiage about conductors and by conductors to give a concise boots-on-the-ground view of the maestro from the orchestra players' viewpoint. It's "soft revenge porn" for the orchestral musician from a musical anthropologist who has spent 40+ years of embedded participant observation.

Finally, I share a few thoughts about the future of orchestras and how to keep this most wonderful of art forms alive and thriving.

A Survival Guide
for Musicians and
Those Who Love Them

Congratulations! You are one of the lucky few to win a position in an orchestra. You entered the field of battle and held your nerves together. (They don't drug test yet for orchestral auditions like they do in other sports so no need to flush your beta blockers.) You vanquished hundreds of other worthy musical combatants and came out on top. Your years of toil and countless hours of preparation have finally borne fruit. You sang your heart out. You played your ass off. You won!

Congratulations!

If you are now one of the 5,000 musicians who plays in a full-time orchestra in the United States, you have attained that rare steady job in music. A middle-class existence is within reach; it's almost safe to contemplate a life as a normal tax-paying citizen. If you are now one of the 70,000 musicians who plays in a part-time or community orchestra, you have just risen to the upper end of the federal poverty scale. But like all those lucky musicians, you deserve a hearty pat on the back... just hope that our dedicated public servants see fit to provide affordable healthcare for the geezers (like me) who make up 90 percent of your fan base. You need us to stay alive for as long as possible.

The future of classical music rests upon the shoulders of talented musicians willing to suffer the trials of securing and keeping a position in an orchestra. Their dedication and artistic integrity must never fade even in the face of the numerous pressures and obstacles. *Orchestra Confidential* is a handbook and field guide that will help musicians stay on course.

"Geography is destiny."
— Anonymous

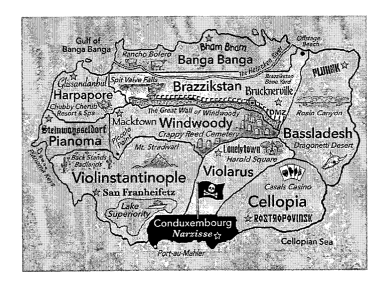

Life in an orchestra is all about geography. Your enjoyment and satisfaction in your new job is directly proportional to where you sit and who sits near you. If the person you sit next to and the people who sit very near to you in the orchestra are agreeable colleagues both musically and personally, you will love your job. It does not matter what musical and interpersonal "horrors" are taking place in other parts of the orchestra, you will be unaffected and uninterested in their suffering.

STRINGS

The History and Nature of String Instruments

The first string instruments were invented around the same time that humans began to hunt with a bow and arrow, around 70,000 years ago. The strings on a stone-age bow that shoots the arrow were made from the tightly wound guts of animals. The strings on a present-day violin are made from the tightly wound guts of a cat — catgut.

The essential design of a violin has not changed much in 70,000 years. Around 10,000 years ago, people began making harps and lyres. A thousand years ago, musicians started to use a bow made of horse or pig hair to slide across a set of strings attached to a resonant wooden box, enabling the instrument to make a continuous tone, a more sustained sound.

Around 500 years ago, violin/string instrument makers began to assemble exquisitely crafted instruments made with specially selected wood which was then treated with a secret varnish, a carefully distilled witch's brew from tightly guarded recipes. A large number of brass players died drinking this varnish; they thought it might help their tone.

The shape of these instruments took on a human form. They looked very much like a sixteenth century ball gown, rounded through the torso, narrow at the waist, wide through the hips. They looked and sounded beautiful. And they became *very* expensive. As I write, in 2018, a middle-of-the-road string instrument will cost as much as an expensive sports car. String instruments are now priced like rare art works. A few years ago, a rare Stradivarius viola sold for $45 million. The aggregate value of all the string instruments in an orchestra—around $5-10 million—is 50 times more than that of all the brass instruments combined. *Violin cases alone are worth more than all that brass plumbing.*

For the novice string player, a word of caution: When you find out that your colleagues in the brass section make more money than you do, your feelings of bitterness at such a grave injustice will almost certainly rise to the surface. This is understandable. Beware, however, that the resentment you feel toward some of your colleagues and *especially toward your greedy violin dealer* may intrude in your thoughts and begin make you a less pleasant person to be around.

If you have the misfortune to sit in the back of the string section and in front of the trumpets and/or trombones, you will soon begin to question why you mortgaged your house to buy that $100,000 fiddle, viola, or cello that you can't hear because you are wearing $500 custom-designed ear plugs *all* the time. If the pungent brew emanating from the bells of the trombone section, a tangy combination of brass fungus, valve oil, garlic mashed potatoes, and two-week-old McDonald's wrappers comes wafting over the stand, resist the urge to use nose plugs. The addition of nose plugs to ear plugs will make you look like you aren't having fun.

The Musicians Who Play String Instruments

Violins come in all shapes and sizes. The modern orchestra employs the four most popular types: violin, slightly oversized violin (viola), violoncello (cello), and bass violin (bass).

There are a lot of string players in the orchestra—usually around 60. An orchestra is only as good as its string section so their job is *the* most critical to the success of any orchestra. String musicians play all the time, every piece on every program—literally hundreds of times more notes than the woodwinds and brass sections.

In addition, string players have to contend

with stand partners. Two musicians sitting side-by-side playing the same notes at the same time creates a highly charged, rapidly changeable micro-climate. Interactions between stand partners are unpredictable—affected by temperature in the hall; distance from the conductor; distance from the music stand; and position in the dyad: outside and closer to the audience, or inside and responsible for page turns. Body odors and perfumes, amplified by close proximity are unhelpful while playing a string instrument. Hearing and smelling only go well together during sex.

The stand partner relationship can be friendly, cooperative, and musically satisfying...or barely tolerable. When all the pressures of playing with a stand partner are combined with the feelings of inadequacy that lurk in all musicians, the result is a highly combustible brew. It can very quickly deteriorate and go from being a fierce competition to a full-blown sado-masochistic emergency.

String players must nevertheless look beyond the imposition of stand partners and put personal feelings aside. The string section has a job to do. Its members are the oarsmen of the orchestra; they row the boat, transporting the golden sounds of genius through stormy seas to the cheering throngs at port.

Advice to String Players

Be a good citizen. Don't lose sight of the fact that playing a string instrument in an orchestra is a not just a gig, it's a calling. *As you toil through page after unrelenting page of increasingly indiscernible black scrawls in the fifth hour of* Siegfried *while your mouth-breathing stand partner sits there barely playing or worse, drooling and having a nervous breakdown, when your shoulder muscles scream in pain and the unsympathetic conductor yells, "faster tremelo!" remember what an indispensable contribution you are making to the orchestra. You did not choose the wrong profession; you are right where you're supposed to be. Resist negative thoughts. However much you may feel like one, you are not a galley slave. Repeat: you are not a galley slave. And remember, the likelihood of finding another job is slim.*

During rehearsals and performances, never turn around and look at the brass section, particularly the trombone section. Avoid eye contact at all times. Trombonists can be easily put off by people who play lots of fast notes, especially if they're hung over (which is often). Check out season 1 of Orange Is the New Black *for tips on the most effective body language to ward off any trouble.*

Violin

Playing the violin (fiddle) is hard. It is the crown jewel of classical music with a sound that is most like the human voice. No instrument can cry like the violin. It can cry like a woman or a man, and it can cry happy or sad.

The violin is equally convincing playing the mischievous rogue, as in Richard Strauss' *Ein Heldenleben* (The Hero's Life), or the dying diva in Puccini's *La Boheme* or Verdi's *La Traviata*. Its sound can challenge or caress. Since the violin can be played both faster and slower and over a wider range than other instruments, composers write music that is more demanding for the violin, requiring violinists to attain a very high level of mastery.

Fiddlers are blessed with the gift of a wonderful repertoire. Violin music by great composers could fill a stadium. Violinists feel a great responsibility to nurture and promote this vast treasure trove of music. They see themselves as "keepers of the flame." It is thus understandable that violinists are musical snobs. They give off an air of entitlement. They look down on the paltry, inferior repertoire of the other orchestral instruments and consider it completely unworthy of even the slightest mention when compared to the magisterial works written for the violin.

Once, while in Tokyo, I thought it was a good idea to bring a well-known violinist to a concert of trumpet and organ music, starring the famous trumpet soloist, Maurice André. At the intermission, my violinist friend turned to me and commented on Mr. André's choice of repertoire, "I don't play transcriptions. I stopped playing silly pieces like that when I was nine-years-old." He then chuckled derisively, got up and left the concert hall.

It is a prerequisite for violinists to begin their studies at a very young age because young supple limbs are required in order to twist the wrist of the left hand rather severely in a clockwise direction, so the fingers will properly align with the fingerboard. It is universally accepted that in order to play the inexhaustible piles of great and fiendishly difficult violin music, violinists must submit to this "musical foot binding."

After the body is suitably aligned, many young players spend their summers at violin camp or string camp where they study the masterpieces written for their instrument: concertos and sonatas, string quartets and chamber music. When violinists get a bit older and move on to conservatory, they continue their studies of solo and small ensemble repertoire but now are required to add a large chunk of orchestra to their schedule. This does not make many students happy at all. They view playing in the orchestra as an intrusion on their time, time which would be better spent digging deeply into a more engaging repertoire, rather than slogging through a Mahler symphony hour after hour with thirty other violinists. They tend not to take orchestra as seriously as their other musical studies. But they will.

Advice for New Violinists

It will come as a great shock to you when you realize that the opportunities to perform the masterpieces from the solo and chamber music violin repertoire, music of profound intimacy, music you have studied your entire life, will be few and far between. As the glory of performing the Brahms violin concerto or touring the world performing the complete Bartók string quartets fades into a haze of what "might have been," or "might have been possible in a just universe," violinists find themselves facing the harsh choice of either cobbling together an "I live for art" musical life, dipping in and out of poverty, or throwing their hat into the ring and auditioning for an orchestra job with its rosy prospect of paying their rent on time.

For those violinists fortunate enough to win a highly coveted position in an orchestra, after the euphoria of receiving a steady pay check wears off and they find themselves doing the backstroke in the orchestra violin pool with thirty other violinists they don't know and often don't care to know, they will more than likely experience a full-blown existential crisis.

The profound realization of what life will be for the next quarter century will hit them like a car crash. They will become acutely aware of their surroundings. They will begin to notice that their stand partner's shaky bow arm and his faint odor of gin are somehow related. The smells emanating from musicians in his geographic area will make a violinist gag. And don't forget about the "sniffers," those stand partners who sniff very loudly on the conductor's upbeat to "help" their partner play at the right time. They will surely cause the partner's body to spasm unpleasantly.

Violinists will become less and less enthralled by the veterans' wistful reveries about "the good old days" of authoritarian, rehabilitated Nazi conductors who "really knew the score" and "really cared about the music." Those cute little old guys who play the first four measures of every concerto on the break will no longer seem cute or charming and will instead engender thoughts of homicide. When a stand partner flips out and starts playing as loudly as possible while muttering in a loud stage whisper expressly so the rest of the section can clearly hear, "these bowings are total shit! Brahms doesn't go like this! Are the concertmaster and conductor doing each other?" the partner will wonder, "How is this even slightly acceptable?"

After a few years in the orchestra, most violinists begin to settle into their new life. They learn to be one of many and how to "go the flow." They adjust to the competitive violin pecking order, the idiosyncrasies of various stand partners, and the intricacies of playing while wearing ear plugs. They will begin to accept that no one cares about their musical ideas and that the conductor doesn't know their name.

However, there are some violinists who never adjust to the relative anonymity of being a small cog in a very big wheel, players who feel they are not appreciated in a manner worthy of their talents. Of course, in all parts of the orchestra, and indeed in every field of endeavor, there are those who feel underappreciated. But, in an orchestra, it is more likely that violinists will suffer this existential angst and feel compelled to express their anger because: 1) there are more violins than any other instrument in the orchestra so it is easier to feel lost in a sea of fiddles than it is in any other section, and 2) violinists are more likely to see themselves as classical music "royalty," one of the chosen few who has ascended to the pinnacle of their art form.

Thus, some are wholly unprepared for their abrupt transition into the general population of the violin section. Since there is no such thing as solitary confinement in an orchestra, their thwarted artistic ambition usually leads to petty arguments with their colleagues over matters like page turns or perfume, with the stage crew over the misplacement of their specially selected chair. They will have episodes of paranoia, like getting into a beef with the garage attendant for letting the air out of their tires, despite not having a shred of evidence. Their significant other will insist they leave the house every day to avoid being around them.

Over time, some fiddlers' anger and frustration can erupt into full blown acts of musical terrorism: practicing the concert master's solos at the break to show everyone how it "really goes," tapping their foot very loudly and out of rhythm to confuse their colleagues sitting close to them, coming in earlier and playing louder than everyone else because everyone else is "too scared to play," and laughing out loud when a colleague makes a mistake.

New violinists should do everything possible to avoid these dyspeptic "revengers." Tell any lie or feign any injury to fend off the prospect of sitting with such a musician. And, violinists who notice they are beginning to act like a revenger, even a little bit, should seek professional help immediately.

Cello

With her elegant curves nestled perfectly between the cellist's open arms and legs in a gentle embrace, the cello has the bearing of a beautiful woman.

The cello fits together perfectly with the human body. It is the most user-friendly instrument to play. It doesn't require the wrist and arm contortions of the violin or viola and it is not unwieldy like the bass. The cello is ergonomically sensible. The cellist plays sitting on the front of chair, back straight in a naturally relaxed posture, chest broad and open, legs spread enough to welcome the instrument, feet planted firmly on the ground. Healthy.

But then there is the problem of transport. All professional cellists have had a fight with an airline employee about taking their cello on the plane, despite having purchased a ticket for the instrument. Imagine being forced to put a $100K instrument in the cargo hold. Imagine retrieving your cello in baggage claim and finding it in two pieces. I've witnessed this catastrophe first hand. It's like watching your house burn down. And if the worry of airport and other forms of public transport were not stressful enough, cellists must walk around town with the thing strapped to their back because cello cases don't have wheels. Plus, rolling a cello along the ground is bad for the instrument because the vibrations can cause cracks in the wood.

Carrying this big heavy thing gives cellists the look of religious penitents bearing a cross. They bear their burden bravely, but after a few years the effort to carry this "small person" around on their backs, it begins to show on their faces. When in a conversation with a cellist, they're liable to get this, "going through this must be very difficult for you..." expression on their face.

Empathetic. Sensitive. Artistic. Cellists cultivate this *look*. The look helps them get into the character of the music they play.

The cello may look like a woman but it sounds like a man. The reassuring dark soulful baritone voice of the cello is the composer's choice to evoke the last hours of a solitary man facing execution (Cavaradosi in *Tosca*), the heart rending losing battles of the tilter at windmills (*Don Quixote*), religious penitents (*Verdi's Requiem*), and big beautiful birds that don't fly much (Saint-Sans, *The Swan*). The cello gives "great empathy." It does "you poor thing" music better than other instruments.

There is always an unspoken competition going on in the cello section for the crown of "most sensitive" or "most artistic." Cellists are the members of the orchestra most likely to cry over a particularly

touching musical passage. Or when the viola section comes in a measure early or if they sit too close to the piccolo player.

About the cello

The cello is the only orchestral instrument that can be played while the musician's head is tilted upward. No other instrument can be played while looking up at the ceiling or looking around the room. Yo-Yo Ma has taken advantage of this peculiarity and incorporated it into his signature move. While playing a particularly soaring melody, he begins to rock side to side in his chair, his head gently swaying left to right. Then, as the music grows in intensity, his head propels skyward, brow knitted, eyes closed, clearly giving the impression he is searching the heavens for inspiration, for a sign from God. This move is $$, a rock star move.

The "head tilt" is key to understanding Yo-Yo Ma's immense popularity. All young cellists should study this move and use it. Managements love the "head tilt." They interpret it as a cellist is really being "into the music." They will arrange to seat such cellists on the stage so they are fully visible to the public. They might even give them a raise. But, while the management may love them, their colleagues will view a "head tilt searching the heavens" move as showboating, like an excessively jubilant, mocking touchdown celebration. It will piss them off. So, use the "head tilt" judiciously.

Bass

In the past thirty years, orchestral bass playing has vastly improved. Back in the day, the bass section sounded like a bunch of large crates being dragged across a wood floor, which regularly elicited "what the hell was that" looks from their colleagues.

Those times are now long gone. Bassists now practice and regularly perform transcriptions of difficult violin and cello music in addition to the one piece composed specifically for the bass, the *Dragonetti Double-Bass Concerto* (you're lucky if you've missed this one). The only people who have actually heard bass players perform these pieces are other bass players.

Thankfully, the bass as a solo instrument never caught on, but all the hours of practice required to play solos that were composed—but that no one cares to hear—has raised the level of orchestral bass playing by orders of magnitude. For the orchestra, all this means is that bassists can now play much louder. Yippie. But they still drag. Bassists fall in love with their tone and play too slowly.

Sometimes the modern confident bass section feels that the cello section needs a little "boost," that the low octave needs a little more "torque,"or needs to be "Bootsy Collins-ed."(the bassist for Parliament-Funkadelic) For a bass player, there is no feeling quite like turbo charging the bass line. Fun for the bass players. No fun for the cellos. The cello section finds these musical slam-dunk contests crude and tasteless. (I confess to a soft spot for tastelessness). They hate being drowned out by overzealous bass sections.They feel such "too loud" playing as an assault not only on them but more importantly, on the music, often lamenting to the bass section (or anyone else who will listen), "It's bad enough you have disrespected me but how can you disrespect Brahms?" Try not to roll your eyes and remember: cellists are a sensitive bunch and take musical matters very seriously.

Since a string bass is the size of a person, orchestra bassists require a separate large room to store their instruments and gear: the bass room. That's where they hunker down to feed and talk slowly to one another. The bass room is guarded by huge metal traveling bass cases as big as Lebron James that line the corridor outside it. On breaks during rehearsals and intermissions at performances, bass players escape to their bass cave, and other members of the orchestra seldom venture near the bass room. Since bass players have less contact with other members of the orchestra, they are able to avoid most of the petty squabbles, trash talking about conductors, management, the viola section, and conversations about boring details of their colleagues' day-to-day lives.

Since they are somewhat separated from the rest of the orchestra, bass players are also not as well known to most of their colleagues. As a rule, in orchestra life, the less people know about a musician, the better that musician is liked and held in high regard: "He's such a nice guy, keeps to himself, just does his job."

For this reason, bass players are usually elected to the orchestra committee. (The orchestra committee negotiates the musicians' contract with management and weighs in on various problems pertaining to the contract and how it affects the musicians). They become representatives of the rank and file.

New bassists

If and when elected to the committee, not only will the bass player become more of a known quantity but he or she will be expected to "do something." But they soon realize that they really don't "do" anything except attend endless committee meetings, which they make longer because they talk as slowly as they play.

Agenda items under consideration often are urgent matters like, "Why does the bus leave so early?" "She's wearing too much perfume and I can't play." "My stand partner keeps moving the music stand," and "Why is the sound check thirty minutes when it says twenty minutes in the contract." The colossal boredom and other members' picayune bullshit will lead to the downward trajectory of a broken marriage and strong drink.

A spin with the orchestra committee is probably in the future of bass rookies, though they should try hard to avoid the temptation of running for a spot. The temporary ego boost of winning election to the committee will endanger members' health, so don't venture too far from the bass room and practice speed talking and tongue twisters. Consider going vegan. It will dial back the testosterone and thus improve the mood of the cello section.

Viola

The viola is an instrument that doesn't quite fit anywhere. It's not a treble or bass clef instrument. It doesn't play high notes or low notes. Rather, it plays in the low middle register, the register where a refrigerator hums, so it is impossible to notate music for the viola in the treble or bass clef. It, thus, gets to have its own clef. It's called viola clef (alto clef) because only the viola plays in this clef. Other instruments visit viola clef on occasion, like the trombone and bassoon, but the viola lives there full time. Violas do on occasion visit the treble clef, but these sojourns are brief and terrifying. Terrifying, because when they play in treble clef, violists can actually be heard, and avoiding the terror that comes with such exposure is precisely the reason violists choose to play the viola.

Violists get no respect. Even though Jimi Hendrix began his musical studies on viola (violists probably don't know this), the viola still has no "street cred." Violists are seen as failed violinists. Of course, this is unfair...mostly. Their most famous piece is a programmatic work by Hector Berlióz: *Harold in Italy*. The viola is the perfect choice to play the part of Harold, a depressed guy who wanders all over Italy looking for some relief from his melancholy.

Harold wants to fit in somewhere, but much like the viola, he can't find his "place." The piece ends in a musical bacchanal with a group of villagers cavorting in a wild drunken orgy, as Harold stands on the sidelines looking on forlorn... Violists: Bless their hearts.

Violists are the butt of thousands of orchestra jokes from all over the world. The joke that sums up their place in the orchestral hierarchy is the one about the orchestra conductor who was having an affair with a violist's wife. During one of their afternoon trysts, after a vigorous bout of lovemaking, the couple fell asleep, neglecting to extinguish their post-coital cigarettes, resulting in the violist's house being burned to the ground. When informed of the full horror of this catastrophe, the violist responded, "Wow! The maestro really went to *my* house!" Bless their hearts.

Violists are taken for granted, treated like comfy old pieces of furniture. The lack of respect they endure binds viola sections closer together than members of other sections. Unity makes strength. Lots of "Harolds" can be a force to be reckoned with.

Most violists seem to have come to terms with their lot. Their lack of career options makes them grateful to be in the orchestra and as a group, they are a rather contented bunch. They usually get along well. More than other sections, they like to do things as a group. Viola unity serves as an antidote to the discrimination and endless viola jokes which grow so tiresome.

Advice for New Violists

Enthusiastically join the group, throw a cupcake party, exchange favorite recipes, share your joys and concerns, and make up your own viola jokes! It will make life in the orchestra a breeze.

WOODWIND INSTRUMENTS

Although the flutes, oboes, clarinets, and bassoons are all considered part of the woodwind section, it is sort of a misnomer. Unlike the brass section, where all the instruments are played by spitting into brass tubing or the string section where all the instruments are played by pulling a bow across four strings, woodwind instruments are each played differently.

Oboists and bassoonists blow into two wooden reeds (double reeds), causing them to vibrate. Clarinetists make one reed vibrate and flutists and piccolo players blow into and across a silver or gold "head joint," the same way someone would blow across the top of a beer bottle to make a hollow sound. Playing the flute requires lots of air, whereas playing an oboe, bassoon, and clarinets requires very little.

Though the mechanics of modern woodwind instruments may differ, the function of the ancient progenitors of all these instruments was the same: to soothe, calm, transfix, seduce, enchant, and entice the listener. Cavemen sat around the fire and played flutes made from animal bones in what surely must have been religious ceremonies or a seduction ritual of some sort. There are stone carvings of what appear to be double reed players serenading the queen in her chambers from 2500 B.C. in ancient Egypt. And of course, we've all seen the iconic images of snake charmers enticing and mesmerizing vipers of all kinds on instruments that are variations of flutes, clarinets and oboes.

There are spats over intonation that flare up from time to time in almost all woodwind sections. But these disputes only partially concern who is sharp and who is flat. Their underlying roots can be traced back to the ancient lineage of the different instruments. Though never stated, the principal flute, oboe, clarinet, and bassoon are enmeshed, albeit unconsciously, in a 5,000-year-old competition for the title of "best seducer" or "enchantress in chief." "Creative intonation," the pitch of an instrument that sounds most favorable in a particular passage, is a valuable tool for the enchantress and can very much affect how successfully the instrument can woo and seduce the listener.

Never forget: intonation is a matter of opinion. And an opinion can be raised or lowered depending on the circumstances.

Oboe

Oboists spend much more time making reeds than actually playing the oboe. They go through this grueling process to make a reed:

a) buy the bamboo for the reed
b) pre-gouge the cane
c) gouge the cane
d) mold the reed by meticulous scraping it with a razor-sharp reed knife
e) tie the two reeds together (oboes are a double reed instrument)
f) chirp a C2 on the reed
g) scrape some more
h) chirp some more
i) soak in water
j) play for a few hours
k) discard reed and
l) begin all over again because ...
reeds last for only a few hours of playing time.

All oboists must have a major nerd component to run the "reed-making ritual" gauntlet three to four times a week. Oboists' endless reed making (essentially rebuilding the instrument every day with each new reed) qualifies all of them for permanent place on the OCD spectrum. Instead of falling out of bed in the morning, drinking a coffee, and practicing for an hour, oboists spend their first waking hours scraping and chirping reeds, molding their two pieces of bamboo into a vehicle for, in the words of a famous oboist, their "noble" tone. Calling an oboe tone "noble" is ridiculous. Aspiring to a noble tone is simply a way for oboists to distance themselves from their instrumental precursors, the *pangi*, the instrument used by snake charmers, and the shawm, a bigger, much louder version of the oboe, akin to a soprano saxophone and used in medieval outdoor debauches.

Oboists are the intonation police of the orchestra. They always want to tune things up. They are the first musicians to suggest having a little "woodwind section rehearsal" that could go on for hours if no one objected. Oboists get very heated with the flute and clarinet sections for playing out-of-tune (usually sharp), and with the bassoons for playing "flarp" (sharp and flat at the same time). Bless their hearts.

Oboists *worship* the tuning box, a small electronic device which sounds A=440 cycles per second with a mechanical electronic sound, a sound that closely resembles the ringing in a shooter's ears after firing a gun without ear protection: wooooooooo. Oboists always keep the tuning box close at hand. The box holds the orchestra strictly accountable. Deviations from the tuning box induce the oboists to call for an "intonation summit conference." This slavish tethering to the box reminds me of the *Star Trek* episode (never aired) where captain Kirk encounters a civilization in a faraway galaxy where a device that sounds a particular pitch controls the minds of all the zombie like inhabitants.

Oboists don't have to be able to play fast tempos particularly well, but they absolutely have to be able to tug at the heart strings on the slow passages. The piercing reedy sound of the oboe has often inspired composers to write slow plaintive melodies for the instrument, as in Richard Strauss' *Don Juan* where the famous oboe solo alternates between playing the part of the pleading seducer and the reluctant seducee. Nothing particularly noble here for either the aggressor or the victim, but certainly a lot of pleading. "Pleading" oboe solos cause oboists to writhe around in their chairs when they play. Writhing is not noble demeanor. For me, the best oboe sounds are not the most noble, but those that most clearly express a musical cry for help. The more convincing that cry, the more successful the oboist.

Advice for New Oboists

Unfortunately, colleagues assume that new members of the oboe section are damaged psychologically from the countless hours of reed making and probably physically impaired as well from all the reed scraping (carpal tunnel syndrome). No matter how hard a newbie tries to hide it... their colleagues have them pegged. They are nerds.

Embrace your nerdiness, never whine or show displeasure about intonation, keep your head down, smile, and just keep scraping reeds. Never put an electronic tuner on your music stand; its presence can be misconstrued. Don't give in to OCD tendencies by suggesting having a woodwind sectional to work out intonation. Remember intonation can only be improved by changing personnel and that is somebody else's job. And just because the orchestra tunes to the oboe (I never really understood this), this fact doesn't make oboists the intonation police. Always keep in mind the humble origins of the instrument as a snake charmer to coax serpents out of urns. This will give you the proper perspective and keep you grounded.

English Horn

An English horn is a larger oboe. It has nothing to do with England. All oboists play some English Horn. *Cor anglais* was misnamed because it was a mispronunciation of "cor angle," the "angle horn," so named because of its unusual bulbous shaped bell. The English horn plays slow meditative solos. Only. A snake charmer for sure. Cor Anglais players all secretly harbor a desire to play the cello....to graduate from snake charming to the more "distinguished" life of a cellist.

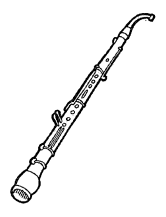

Flutes of All Types

The most famous flutist of all time is the god Pan: part man, part goat, harbinger of spring and fecundity, oversexed lord of the forest, unflagging seducer who spread his seed wherever and with whomever he could. Half man, half goat (cabròn), Pan tootled his reed flute in celebration of all of earth's ecstatic creations. Pan was a god who was 100 percent of this earth. He was not worshipped in temples but in more rustic settings such as caves and grottoes. At the beginning of the twentieth century, French Romantic composers, Debussy and Ravel being the most notable, wrote beautiful music for the flute that sublimates Pan's goat half and brings to the fore his more affable half. It is music that could be described as effervescently seductive.

Romantic composers choose flutes to play frolicking nymphs, birds, butterflies, fauns, and waterfalls. Debussy's *Afternoon of a Faun*, and Ravel's *Daphnis and Chloe* are notable examples of this music. Movie music composers always write bamboo flute music in the background for bucolic scenes of Japanese or Chinese villages. Flutists often play concerts of consoling and angelic music with harps. Flutes do "flirtatious," "cute," and "adorable" way better than other instruments. And they can also do "crazy." Because they play a lot of high fast notes, flutists have been stereotyped as being high strung. As with all stereotypes, this may be only partially true, but the flute does seem to attract people with excitable personalities. Women who play the flute tend to overdress. Men who play the flute suffer from constantly being around well-dressed, high-strung women. The marriage of flute with "high strung" is on display most famously in the iconic "mad scene" from Donizetti's opera, *Lucia di Lammermoor*. In one of opera's most famous meltdowns, the flute introduces a completely distraught Lucia as she staggers onto the stage. Throughout the twenty-minute scene, the flute shadows Lucia's delusional hysteria and exploding brain cells in an epic post-homicidal (she just killed her husband) plunge into madness. Of course, Lucia dies and her boyfriend kills himself. Talk about high strung.

But flutists are generally an affable bunch: they sport an outgoing, gregarious, upbeat, and optimistic persona. They tend to congregate in large numbers at flute conventions and flute competitions, which are always high-energy affairs fueled by a combustible confection of *bon homie, faux* supportiveness, and fierce competition. Flutists buzz around these conclaves sampling the fare on the "menu," like bees fluttering from flower to flower on a honey high, gorging on the seemingly endless bounty of high and fast notes. And always with stingers at the ready....

At these pow-wows, they play flute music with and for each other on flutes of all kinds: piccolos; alto flutes; bass flutes (inaudible unless played alone in a small room); flutes made of platinum, gold, silver, ebony, and bamboo; shakuhachi flutes that need to be submersed in water; and even stone-age flutes made from wooly mammoth tusks. Exhausting. When away from flute gatherings, flutists rarely hang out with other flutists. They need to decompress. They need to be alone.

Advice for New Flutists

New flute players are usually made to feel right at home by their colleagues. Their affable and energetic demeanor and optimistic attitude will surely be a welcome ray of sunshine to the crew of the surrounding jaded orchestra veterans.

But beware that over time your initial ebullience and "happy happy" may begin to wear thin. Though they may not say it aloud, colleagues could start to think, "WTF is she so happy about, we've got to rehearse four hours of Phillip Glass!" Newbies shouldn't worry about this reaction, though: you should stick to your guns. A positive attitude will carry the day.

If you feel too much negative energy coming your way, run for a spot on the orchestra committee, thereby proving to more disgruntled colleagues that you are one of them, that newbies feel their pain. Don't worry about actually having to sit on the committee since "sun reflecting on the spray from a waterfall" personality makes it unlikely that you will get elected.

Advice for New Piccolo Players

Since all flutists have played the piccolo in their lives, you know that flutists generally find the piccolo to be an undignified instrument, something to be toodled in a marching band, a necessary evil in the orchestra. Thus, you may be hated by other orchestra members and even your colleagues in the flute section will just tolerate you. To ward off rejection, defend your territory! Fire a warning shot: Play a particularly shrill passage as loudly as possible. Channel a lead trumpet player. This will not win you any friends but it will earn the respect of your colleagues. Take Al Capone's words to heart: "It's better they fear you than love you." But from time to time, put little chocolates and candies on the stands of people who sit near you. Once in a while, a tasty peace offering won't hurt.

One last thing

Flutists: do not date anyone who plays a treble clef instrument, with the possible rare exception of a very easy going clarinetist who sits right behind you. Restrict your romantic choices to those who play bass clef instruments. Flutists are more successful in their love life if they reserve their ardor for musicians whose instruments resound naturally in the low and middle registers, instruments which comfortably "reside" in a different part of the harmonic series. Trombonists and cellists are good choices. Their overtones will never clash with yours...in music and in life.

Clarinet

The most famous clarinetist ever, Benny Goodman, the "king of swing," was a classically trained Jewish jazz musician. His clarinet playing was the perfect synthesis of classical, jazz, and klezmer (eastern European Jewish party music) clarinet styles. His sound was brilliant and soulful, his technique virtuosic. Goodman's playing was extroverted, playful, soulful. He bent and smeared notes; he used lots of vibrato.

Twentieth century composers were intrigued by this puckish clarinet style perfected by Goodman. In the beginning of Gershwin's "Rhapsody in Blue" the greasy clarinet glissando drops us right into the middle of a scene from the Jazz Age for a raucous night on the town. Stravinsky, Copland, and Bernstein wrote concertos for this impish instrument. But the jazz/classical/klezmer clarinet style of clarinet playing is a relatively new development (over only the last eighty years!) For most of its history in the orchestra, as part of the woodwind section, the clarinet played with a darker, more reserved aristocratic tone. Absolutely no smears and no vibrato.

Eighteenth and nineteenth century composers loved this more traditional "aristocratic" clarinet tone for its hollow, organ pipe sound. In comparison with the brilliant clarinet stylings of the jazz era, this restrained vibrato-less clarinet sound was a blank canvas on which anything could be painted. Since it betrayed so very little emotion, the clarinet became composer's "go to" instrument for expressing existential angst. The clarinet was perfect for portraying lonely and forsaken. Schubert chose the clarinet to be the lonely shepherd in his famous song cycle, "Shepherd on a Rock," composed near the end of his life. Puccini picked the clarinet for Cavaradossi's jail cell lament about his impending execution at the beginning of the third act of *Tosca*.

Verdi featured the clarinet in the famous aria from *La Forza del Destino*, "O tu che in seno agli angeli," which contains the famous line, "Life is hell to those who are unhappy."

As a group, clarinet players are more cognizant of the wider musical universe, and more versatile than other orchestra members. Most clarinetists have played in a polka band at least once. Unlike their colleagues in the woodwind section, there is a good chance that orchestral clarinetists actually know who Eric Dolphy or Peanuts Hucko was. They are more likely to play other instruments, to "double" on saxophone and flute.

Clarinetists usually have more friends in other sections of the orchestra than their colleagues in the woodwind section. Their musical worldliness makes them more empathetic toward their colleagues. It gives them a reassuring, almost avuncular presence compared with flutists, oboists, and bassoonists.

Clarinetists tend to have a "look." They are bent over ever so slightly at the waist, and their shoulders are rounded a little like they are about to wrap their shorter and stubbier than average fingers around a licorice stick. When they smile there is always a hardly noticeable indentation on the top of their lower teeth because they have been worn away by the pressure of the clarinet mouthpiece. Clarinetists would be easy to pick out of a lineup.

Clarinetists writhe around when they play. They're always moving their shoulders up and down, bending forwards and backwards from the waist, rotating their necks, moving the clarinet around in circles. I've always found all this movement rather odd. Playing a clarinet is not as physically demanding as a brass instrument or even a cello; physical force or "body English" of any kind is not necessary in clarinet playing. So why the gyrations? I used to think that these spastic tics were simply a byproduct of musicians expressing "lonely and forsaken," an involuntary physical response to music evoking angst. But recently I've come around to thinking that the clarinetist's herky-jerky movements are really the outward physical manifestation of their fierce internal battle to keep their mischievous impish rogue, the ever-lurking jazz/klezmer/polka band clarinet demon, from escaping and killing their fragile "lonely and forsaken" persona. Just a thought.

Bass clarinet

The bass clarinet is the coolest instrument in the orchestra. So it has always puzzled me why bass clarinetists are such nerds. They all dress like high school basketball coaches and a harbor secret desire to be principal clarinet. Wake up guys! Eric Dolphy played the bass clarinet. Bass clarinet is cool! Buy some new clothes and move your chair six inches farther away from the rest of the clarinet section. Be the star you are!

Advice for All Clarinetists

Clarinetists who are not the principal should please sit still! Leave the davening *to the principal clarinetist. Clarinetists who come in as principal should remember that only other clarinetists are impressed by all the moving around; it only makes other colleagues roll their eyes. No one cares how high and super soft a clarinetist can play. Colleagues think, "Why the hell can't they just sit still and play and why are they playing so damn soft?" Sing it out. Free the Klezmer!*

Flute and bassoon sections will likely appreciate your levelheadedness and you very likely will need their support when inevitably the oboe section begins "policing" the intonation. Remember that clarinetists have much more technique than any oboist and should use every opportunity to demonstrate this fact. In the fast woodwind tutti *passages, be sure to rush a tiny bit and play a tiny bit louder than would be considered good taste. Tap a foot loudly. This is like peeing around the perimeter of clarinetist territory.*

Don't sell your saxophone. You can make some extra money in the orchestra playing the very occasional saxophone part that pops up from time to time. And it gives you street cred with non- musicians.

Bassoon

Faggoto (Italian meaning "stick"). Unfortunately, the often-used Italian word for bassoon is currently forbidden to be spoken in the United States because of its affront to the LGBTQ community.

The bassoon is an interesting instrument. Consider that the price of a bassoon is about the same as a luxury car—and ten times what a trumpet costs. All bassoonists play a bassoon made by the *same* family. Bassoonists have played only Heckel bassoons for almost 200 years! The Heckel family runs a small Santa's workshop operation in Germany and the wait time to get a new bassoon is literally years. No wonder there are fewer bassoon in the world than any other band or orchestral instrument.

The bassoon is the least sexy instrument of the orchestra. It looks and sounds like a belching bedpost. Other musicians and civilians alike silently wonder, "Why in God's name did you choose to play the bassoon?" When Haydn first heard a bassoon he is reported to have said, "Thank God it doth not smell."

Bassoonists look more ridiculous than even bagpipers. At least bagpipers play standing up, wear colorful clothes, and can play louder than mezzo piano.

In Russia, failed trumpet players with collapsed embouchures were encouraged to play the bassoon. But even with Russian passion, people aren't moved to tears by bassoon music, unless they are tears of laughter. Just because Mozart wrote a concerto for the bassoon when he was eighteen doesn't change the instrument's appeal. His is only one piece of music composed especially for bassoon in the last 250 years that anyone might know.

Bassoon music within a score often depicts old men (grandpa in *Peter and the Wolf* and the old storyteller in *Scheherazade*), a exhausted mother singing to her baby (Stravinsky's *Firebird*), a creature rising out of primordial goo (*Le Sacre du Printemps*), ridiculous villains (the Lex Luther theme in *Superman* movies), or any character in a sitcom or cartoon who is just plain goofy (a dog driving a bus or the principal leaving a school board meeting unaware she has a sign on her back that reads, "Never trust a fart").

But joking aside, the bassoons are the anchor of the woodwind section. They play the bass part. Good bassoonists have excellent "time," like good jazz bass players. If the bassoons are bad, the woodwind section falls apart.

Advice for New Bassoonists

New bassoonists should remember that when bassoons are good, the woodwind section is happy. Colleagues in the woodwind section appreciate and value the contribution of a good bassoonist. They will show you the respect a wealthy employer shows a particularly able member of her staff, like the gardener. They will appreciate you the way a quarterback appreciates his offensive line for risking traumatic brain injury to keep him safe and sound. Accept the class distinctions. Bassoonists are loved.

Contra Bassoon

A contra bassoon is more of a sound effect than an instrument, with contra bassoons sounding like a portable generator about to die. The pitches on a contra bassoon are not distinguishable. New contra players specifically should record a Christmas album to hand out to colleagues to demonstrate the extraordinary musical possibilities of the contra that no one ever considered before. Colleagues will congratulate you for great work and smile at you as they would smile at a small child showing her mom a good report card. But no one will ever listen to your album. Don't despair. Remember, payday is Thursday.

BRASS INSTRUMENTS

All brass instruments are essentially trumpets with brass tubing of different lengths. The hard brass (trumpets and trombones) are the only orchestral instruments that can be pointed like a gun directly at something or someone: the back wall, a chandelier, a violist's head, the conductor. Brass players even talk about their instruments the way gun owners talk about guns: bore size, muzzle velocity (high notes), throat size/bullet molds (mouthpieces).

The brass section, particularly the musicians who play the hard-brass instruments (trumpets and trombones/tuba), are mutterers, always grumbling about something. Since they sit in the back of the orchestra, their grumbles are inaudible to the conductor and the conductor's words of wisdom to the string section are often inaudible to the brass section. This often leads to misunderstandings and resentment for both parties. When the conductor does speak to the trumpets and trombone players, it is usually to tell them they are playing too loud. True to form, the hard brass reacts ·by grumbling pithy expressions of discontent, "That was my *mezzo forte, asshole,"* and the cycle repeats itself *ad infinitum*.

French horn players are the weirdos of the brass section. They do stuff like go to cheese eating/livestock auctions in remote Alpine villages where they blow their Alphorns (an unwieldy straight eight-foot long wooden tube which was used to communicate across mountain passes in the days before the telephone) to entertain the animals and the cheese eaters. Experienced conductors don't say much to the French horn players because they know that if their words are not chosen very carefully, they could trigger a mental breakdown. More about this later.

Advice for New Brass Section Musicians

Be aware that muttering is fine, but be sure to smile and nod your head in affirmation when the conductor is speaking even if you cannot hear him or her or do not agree with a single word spoken.

Advice for Female Brass Musicians

Sadly, you need to face the fact that the brass section has been a man's world for a long time. You are greatly outnumbered there. In fact, no doubt, you have had to deal with the male brass players' hypermasculine 'bros club' since you began playing in youth bands and orchestras. While you likely already have developed your own way of navigating the 'bro' universe, you must always deal with the fact that most men with brass instruments in their hands are unlikely to be "woke" any time soon. So until women make up a larger percentage of the brass section (things are trending strongly this way) here, from an old white guy is my humble advice: Don't complain, don't cry when you're pissed off, play your ass off, don't take any shit! And if you are confronted with excessive "mansplaining", consider responding with a random male cliché-like mantra like, "how 'bout dem Steelers!". This kind of response works well in a wide assortment of 'mansplaining' circumstances. The repetition and randomness will keep the guys off balance and can often neutralize an uncomfortable situation.

Trumpet

The trumpet is the instrument of angels and kings. It has been announcing the arrival and departure of the supposedly most important among us for millennia. From earliest recorded history, the trumpet has been associated with kings. Indeed, two trumpets were discovered in ancient Egypt in the tomb of King Tutankhamen—one of silver, one of copper—one to signal his departure from this world and the other to announce his arrival in the next. The Old Testament refers to the trumpet eighty-three times. It even describes in some detail the trumpet calls used in battle: a call to assembly, a call to retreat, and a call to "massacre." In the New Testament, the trumpet gets "kicked upstairs," so to speak, when the angel Gabriel blows his terrifying introduction for you know who....

In the first Olympic games in ancient Athens, there was a trumpet event! It was essentially weight lifting with a trumpet. As the all-male crowd sat and watched, the naked trumpet contestants (all contestants for all events were naked...oh those Greeks!) stood in the center of the arena and blew a trumpet as loudly as possible. The man who blew the loudest blast won the olive wreath. This Olympic trumpet toot off had a practical purpose in ancient

Greece: trumpet signals had to be clearly audible on the battlefield.

Not much has changed in the 2500 years since the first Olympic games.

The music the trumpet plays in the orchestra, the vast majority of the time, is deeply rooted in its military history. When I joined the Metropolitan Opera orchestra, the first thing I was told by the legendary principal trumpeter, Mel Broiles, was, "Always keep this clearly in mind, Mark: Men die in battle to the sound of the trumpet."

Bugle calls, fanfares, marches, battle whoops and signals, proclamations of the arrival and departure of an endless parade of luminaries comprise the trumpeter's gig. These myriad trumpet duties could be listed under the more general job description: "Okay folks, listen up, time to pay serious attention, your life may depend on it."

Throughout the seventeen hours of Wagner's *Ring* cycle, the trumpet "acts" the part of the sword, not just any sword but *the* sword, Siegmund and Siegfried's sword, the blade stuck in a tree for centuries. The mythical sword is a perfect metaphor for the trumpet sound. The razor-sharp sword, like the pure penetrating sound of the trumpet, severs the head cleanly from the neck. No bullets or bludgeons. No explosions or thumping, just the whoosh of steel traversing the air on its way to tidy decapitation. Anyone who sits in front of the trumpets understands this conflation.

There was once a principal trumpet player whose section referred to him as "Fearless Leader." This designation was both a grudging show of respect and a sarcastic jibe. All members of the section knew that they were better trumpet players than the principal trumpet but everyone also knew that they were not smarter or better informed musically than the Fearless Leader. But he tended his flock well. He happily welcomed all musical suggestions and since the section was comprised of such fine players, he made sure his charges had enough to play to both keep everyone happy, which greatly reduced his workload. Fearless Leader is now enjoying his retirement tending his herb garden and playing badminton with his lovely young wife.

John Williams loves the trumpet. He uses the instrument to recall the bravery and sacrifice of soldiers on the beaches of Normandy in "Summon the Heroes," to reflect Lincoln's wartime struggles during the Civil War, and to accompany any serious ass kicking (there is always ass kicking in a movie with a John Williams score).

Trumpet players can become too fond of testosterone-saturated trumpet parts, like those in John Williams movies. Overexposure to heroic trumpet music can cause a chemical imbalance which can lead to a neurological disorder called Star Wars Syndrome. This is a uniquely male disorder. When women become more prominent in orchestra trumpet sections, the next iteration of *Orchestra Confidential* might have a section in it discussing how some female trumpeters have succumbed to "Kill Bill" Syndrome (alluding to a movie with a badass female lead with a kickass trumpet dominated soundtrack).

When a trumpeter plays heroic trumpet parts, the neural pathways connecting the pubic region in front of the scrotum and behind the umbilicus to the lizard brain (medulla oblongata) are "lit up," opened to maximum "bandwidth." The pubic region and the lizard brain join forces, becoming best friends so to speak, and begin an assault on the trumpeter's cerebral cortex, causing disorientation and great confusion.

The trumpeter has great difficulty distinguishing between "music life" and "non-music life." He convinces himself he is not the paunchy, out-of-shape suburbanite father of three chasing his kids around Chuck E. Cheese, but rather, he sees himself as a dashing trumpet-toting Hans Solo, roaming the galaxy while slicing the forces of evil to pieces with his magic trumpet sword. All orchestra trumpet players suffer from Star Wars Syndrome to some degree. Milder cases of are often accompanied by purchase of a fast car, wearing too tight clothes, and/or watching loops of Red Bull extreme sports/suicide mission videos at every orchestra break. In these milder cases, the afflicted trumpeter can be brought back into the real world by someone in the brass section who can take him aside, look directly in his eyes and say some version of, "Hey, asshole, grow up!" It is usually more effective if a female brass player carries this message.

In extreme cases of Star Wars Syndrome, trumpeters see themselves not just as a "trumpet hero" but a *wronged* trumpet hero. This devolution occurs when a trumpeter who has suffered through a few egregious mishaps in some particularly exposed trumpet solos, doubles down. Such trumpeters begin playing much much louder, obsessively asking colleagues in the brass section, "Ya think it's loud enough, ya think it's projecting?" They begin using a bigger, heavier instrument, start lining up ten mouthpieces at a time on their stand, testing them to see if they can get the string players in the front of the orchestra, not just those in his close proximity, to use earplugs.

Wronged trumpet heroes suffer bouts of rage. They isolate themselves. They get pissed that jazz trumpet players are more famous than they are even though orchestra trumpeters play with a bigger sound. They mumble to themselves about how their fearlessness and leadership are not appreciated. Before concerts, they are overheard reciting the war cry of the great Indian warrior, Crazy Horse: "Today is a good day to die!" They decide that they have to take things into their own hands, that they alone can fix things. They think they overhear their colleagues talking about the small size of their hands and feet... they have gone "Full Rambo." There is no cure for this.

Advice for New Trumpeters

Keep in mind that the trumpet's military genealogy inevitably leads some principal trumpet players to want to play the part of a general. Thus, if led by a "general" you should do the following:

1) refrain from playing louder than the general

2) come in no earlier than the general

3) remember that the general is always in tune

4) speak only when spoken to, should the general go Full Rambo, and then offer only words of encouragement, like "Wow! That was fucking loud! What projection!" and

5) bring coffee to rehearsal once a week.

Advice for New Principal Trumpeters

Do not say much to your section but listen to what members have to say. Stand up when asking the conductor a question. And never sit in front of the trombones. Do not take in too much new information; it will only be confusing and cause a loss of nerve.

Oscar Levant has solid advice for lead trumpeters: "I've given up reading books. I find it takes my mind off myself." Time for contemplation is over! You play lead trumpet! Stay focused! On yourself! Lead the band! You are the tip of the spear. "Today is a good day to die."

French Horn

The French horn is a twelve-foot-long brass tube, shaped like a cone, that is wound around and around like intestines. The tube finally ends in a very large bell. There are horns where the tubing is straightened out, all twelve feet of it. This is the alpine horn. It is played by Swiss guys in lederhosen in the mountains to signal their friends across the valley. It sounds awful.

Twelve feet from mouth to fundament (the bell) is a long way for sound to travel. The bell of the French horn sits on the player's thigh and directs the sound away from the audience toward the back wall of the concert hall. In order to manipulate the intonation and tone color, the player's right hand is placed in the bell, coaxing warm chocolatey tones out of the horn's labyrinthine brass intestines. The horn's dark diffuse sound vibrates the inner organs of both the horn player's and the listener's body. For the listener, the wide array of high and low overtones offers a gentle massage from collar bone to pubic bone. The horn sound is reassuring. For the horn player, since the sound is produced so close to body, it traumatizes the inner organs, which often leads to mental health problems later in life.

Composers love the French horn. Mozart wrote

four concertos and Richard Strauss wrote two concertos for it. Composers expect French horn players to do everything: use an "indoor" voice and an "outdoor" voice; play many different characters, both male and female; wear many costumes and hats, sometimes all in the same piece. Players should be the fearless young hero at the beginning of the piece, the conquering hero in the middle, and reminiscing dying hero at the end of the piece. Further, while in between those heroic episodes, they should be the comfy magic carpet for the woodwind section to float their disparate sounds on, and then be ready to hold down the PAH in the OOM-PAH whenever there is an OOM-PAH passage.

Horn players think they have the hardest job in the orchestra. They won't often say this out loud but people can see it in their eyes, that look of suffering superiority, that "I know what combat's all about and you don't" look. French horn players wear their "woe is me, my instrument is so hard" as a badge of honor. They see themselves as soldiers on the musical frontlines, dodging the bullets and shrapnel shot out of their own bells.

Musicians in other sections are not usually sympathetic to the travails of the horn section, though they might acknowledge how difficult a French horn player's job is if they thought about it, which they probably will not. At the end of the day French horn players' colleagues don't give a shit how hard their job is.

The performance pressure of having to play all those different characters and keep them sorted out in their head makes horn players jumpy and skittish. They all show clear signs of PTSD. Horn players can usually keep it together until around age fifty. After that, when they hit a rough patch and have a few performances where things don't go exactly as planned, they are prone to long bouts of depression. They've taken a few too many punches. They go fucking nuts. Therefore, their colleagues and the conductor would be well advised to treat horn players with great delicacy. They shouldn't ever look at horn players while they have their instruments in their hand and choose their words carefully when speaking to them, not saying anything to spook them. Be reassuring and calm. Interact with them as you would with the field goal kicker for an NFL team sitting alone at the end of the bench. Treat them as you would a functional mental patient.

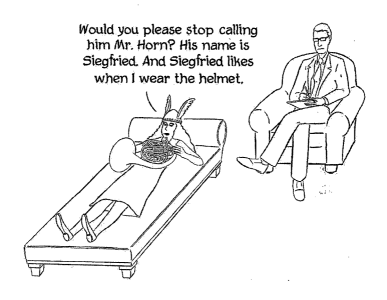

In a perfect world

Horn players fall into two broad categories, the "Siegfrieds" (the fearless hero) and the "Engineers" (the cautious calculator)." A pure Siegfried will run into a burning building without hesitation, resulting in either "superherodom" or a moving eulogy. A pure Engineer will construct a timeline of when the burning building will likely be completely consumed by flames, do a quick calculation, and then decide what to do. Most horn players are a hybrid Siegfried/Engineer. Pure Siegfrieds don't hang around for long. If they continue in music, they most likely would be found playing in a prog metal band.

In a perfect world, where money is no object, an orchestral horn section would best be constructed like a major league pitching staff. The starting pitchers (principal players) would be hybrids, 70 percent Siegfried/ 30 percent Engineer. The middle relievers (section players) would be 60 percent Engineer/40 percent Siegfried. The closer would be 90 percent Siegfried/10 percent Engineer. There is no closer in an orchestral horn section, but there should be. It would be so satisfying to bring this specialist out on stage when a few "high hard ones" are needed in the closing innings, at the end of a symphony.

New hornists should ask themselves: "What kind of French horn player are you?"

Trombone

The trombone is a bigger, more primitive trumpet. Its name is a variation on the Italian words for trumpet, tromba, and "one," meaning large. Since its sound is not impeded by valves like a trumpet, a trombone is able to play much louder than other brass instruments. The bass trombone is practically identical to the tenor trombone, except that it has a bigger bore and uses a bigger mouthpiece. Sounds from a bass trombone add some splash to the lower notes played by the trombone section overall. If trumpets and trombones were firearms, a trumpet would be a sniper rifle, a trombone a grenade launcher.

The modern trombone is a relatively new development, evolving from the fifteenth century instrument, the "sackbut" (admittedly an unfortunate name). Sackbut players had a relatively cushy gig compared to trumpet players because they were exempt from battlefield duty. Since the sackbut requires two hands to play, one to move the slide and one to hold the instrument, unlike the trumpet which can be played one handed, it couldn't be played on horseback, making the sackbut useless as a tool for battlefield communication. Sackbut players were exempted from the trumpeter's treacherous job of sounding the battle charge and retreat, and signaling other troop movements, a job that essentially put a target on the trumpeter's back. While trumpeters were taking their life in their hands, not knowing if their next note would be their very last, the sackbut players were back at the castle chillin', eating root vegetables and drinking beer. Trombone and beer drinking form a sacred union, a tradition that has been faithfully nurtured and kept alive right up to the present day.

The sound of a chorus of trombones playing chorales is the closest that instrumentalists can come to imitating the deep sonorous voice of a wise man, a prophet, a benevolent deity. The sustained tones of lots of trombones playing slow-moving triads, stacking their overtones, creating a "wall" of puffy sound clouds on which the prophet will stand and proclaim is inspiring in its nobility.

Mozart, Brahms, and Bruckner wrote beautiful chorales for the trombone section. Trombone players practice chorales any chance they get, carefully tuning and blending their sounds together. It's a very meditative practice, very Zen, and when played on stage during an orchestra break, very annoying. Other orchestra musicians, relaxing on their break, enjoying their too brief a respite from orchestral sounds, don't hear anything noble or Zen when the trombones are tuning chords; they hear the lugubrious sounds of a group of old men moaning.

The reason why the trombone section plays on the break is because trombonists play so sporadically during rehearsals and concerts. Unlike the string section, the low brass gets to take weeks off because composers didn't always write a trombone part. So trombonists play whenever they can, either on stage or backstage, to stay loosened up, like relief pitchers.

Orchestral chorales are few and far between in the orchestral repertoire. The other half of the trombone section's responsibility, playing the flip side of the benevolent deity, the "pissed-off prophet," Darth Vader-like characters, the Valkyries, etc., doesn't make an appearance that often either. Trombone sections spend a lot of time just sitting still. But when the pissed-off prophet finally does appear in Bruckner, Wagner, or Shostakovich, and the trombone section has the opportunity to do "angry" or "wrath," its musicians' pent-up boredom and frustration explode out of their bells, compelling those unfortunates who sit in front of them to involuntarily reach for their earplugs. There are musicians in the orchestra, and very often even the conductor, who feel that the section overdoes the Darth Vader rage thing, that its gradations of the loud dynamics are undifferentiated and lack subtlety, that they play with excessive exuberance. Or simply stated, they play too fucking loud. Trombonists don't ever agree with that assessment.

Conductors rarely look at the trombone section because they don't want to encourage it. They fear trombone's fire power. In ten years, a conductor might tell the trombone section to play louder three times total, but they will tell the section to play softer at least once a week.

Advice for New Trombonists

Let go of your animosity toward conductors, and do not take anything they say to you individually or to the trombone section personally. When a conductor tells you that you are playing too loud, don't take it as criticism: just think of it as a benediction which conductors have been bestowing on trombonists for as long as there have been orchestras. This old script, "Trombones, I know the passage is marked fortissimo *but I think* mezzo forte *is sufficient," is an ancient orchestral incantation, part of the great tradition of conductor aphorisms. Just be grateful you have received the conductor's benediction. So, whenever the conductor speaks to you, say nothing, don't mutter profanities, don't put on your "perp stare." Just smile and nod assent. Then put your head down and dream about an upcoming performance of Bruckner 4, or go back to playing fantasy football on your phone.*

Tuba

It takes a lot of air to play a tuba. A tuba player must breathe in and blow out tremendous amounts of air. Breathe in very fast. Blow out at just the right speed. Great tuba players are like great bass players. They know when to lead from the bottom. A great orchestra tuba player anchors the bottom and "organizes" the overtones of the brass section and makes the trumpets shine.

Since there is only one tuba per orchestra, the opportunities for getting a job playing tuba in an orchestra are scarce. When there is an opening, tuba "smoke signals" are huffed into the tuba matrix alerting the tribe that the next big tuba toot-off is drawing near. All over the world, hundreds of worthy combatants begin training for the upcoming showdown. Tuba elders are sought out for their musical wisdom and training secrets as the contestants diligently prepare for battle. When the eventual winner is crowned, the tribe broadcasts a collective cheer and the tuba eruption dies down. The tribe goes back to mining low notes.

As you might imagine, the winner of a tuba audition has to be a real badass. Ninety percent of tubists in orchestras are able to play the Khachaturian violin concerto and all six Bach cello suites....on the tuba. Listening to tubists play these transcriptions is like watching elephants play Frisbee. Since such virtuosity is not part of the job description of an orchestra tuba player, the fact is that orchestra tuba players are way overqualified. For all the rigorous preparation and brutal competition they must endure to get a spot in an orchestra, the winner of a tuba audition essentially secures a spot in a very comfy musical retirement home. Tubists have even less to play than even the trombonists. Once in a while they get to play a solo portraying a lumbering bear or waking dragon but mostly tubists must be content to plant brass "depth charges" and love playing the root of gigantic brass chords.

The only musicians in the orchestra who pay much attention to the tuba are the trombonists and wise first trumpet players. They are the only ones who notice when the tuba is even slightly out of tune or out of balance with them. Even if one of the trombones is responsible for a particularly out-of-tune low brass chord, the tuba player is often made the convenient scapegoat for the sourness. And usually the tuba player happily accepts the blame, realizing that since the trombone section is forever blending and tuning chords anyway, its members will surely want to run through the nasty-sounding section a few times, and the problem is certain to be sorted out quite amicably.

So…no problem. Harmony restored. Time for a few beers.

Tubists tend to get bored with their not too challenging orchestral repertoire so they find ways other than practicing tuba music to entertain themselves. Since tubists don't ever get to hear the sound of another tuba (remember there is only one per orchestra), they long for contact with another member of the tribe. Thus, they are liable to call up one of their tuba playing buddies so they can play songs for each other over the phone, or experiment with the older precursors to the tuba, the *bombardone* (the name says it all) and the *serpent* (twelve feet of brass tubing bent into the shape of a snake and sounding like a snake).

Many begin testing their physical limits by playing bigger and bigger tubas until they have successfully simulated the sound of a 707 taking off. This "extreme sport" may cause seizures or, in the best case, bring on a bout of lock jaw or Bell's Palsy. Some of the more staid or cerebral tuba players may learn a foreign language or take up the guitar to fill in all their spare time.

Tuba players are a very easy-going lot. They are usually unassuming and reluctant to do anything that might call attention to themselves. Since the bell of a tuba points straight up in the air, they can't easily point it at anyone to inflict pain and thus never incur the ire of those sitting in front of them. Al Mennuti was the tuba player at the Metropolitan Opera in the 1940s and 1950s. His father, Al Mennuti Sr., was president of the New York Musician's Union, Local 802. During intermissions, Mennuti sat in his instrument locker, a space four feet-by-three feet-by five feet high, closed the door, sat on a stool, turned on a little lantern hanging on a clothes hook, and read magazines. He found avoiding all human interaction to be very relaxing. The tuba player has the best job in the orchestra.

PERCUSSION INSTRUMENTS

"In the beginning was the drum..." Indeed, the drum was the first instrument. Humans have played drums everywhere on earth from the time homo sapiens began to walk upright. And now, we really live in the age of the drum. Legions of music producers roam the earth and cyberspace collecting and sampling every drum sound and rhythm they can dig up. Then they integrate these sounds with other sounds they've captured to make "new" beats and grooves, to keep everyone everywhere dancing in the world of instant everything.

In the vast world of drumming, an orchestral percussion section is a city state. Percussionists live at the back of the stage, far from the audience, walled off from the rest of the orchestra by the brass section. They walk around back there moving from instrument to instrument, first playing a few notes on the xylophone, then smacking the tam-tam a couple of times. Next they sit down and tell one of their compatriots a private little joke, then they climb up on a ladder to hit a giant chime... once...and then they sit back down again. Since they are the only musicians moving on the stage, the audience's attention is drawn to the percussion section whose members look to be having a grand old time. Audience members watch the percussion section and think to themselves, "I could do that." That's unlikely.

Before this area of the orchestra was called the "percussion section," it was commonly referred to as the drum section. The drum section begat the percussion section in the second quarter of the twentieth century, right around time of humankind's most profound, literally earth shattering scientific breakthroughs: quantum physics, the Hubble telescope, the theory of general relativity, the talking picture, and the atomic bomb. The father of the percussion ensemble, the "futurist" French composer, Edgar Varèse, understood that a new soundtrack was needed for the brave new world of quanta and quarks. Varèse wrote very percussion-centric music, using the full array of percussion instruments, some of which had never been heard before, in pieces with names like, "Ionization," "Integrales," and "Hyperprisms."

"Ionization" (a five minute piece!) uses all these percussion instruments: tenor drums, snare drums, tarole (a type of piccolo snare drum), bongos, tambourine, field drum, crash cymbal, suspended cymbals, gong, anvils, triangles, sleigh bells, cowbell, chimes, glockenspiel, temple blocks, claves, maracas, castanets, whip, guiro, sirens, lion's roar.

Nineteenth century Romantic heroes were left behind. Scientific phenomena, the new heroes—telescopes, microscopes, molecular configurations and subatomic particles—required a new groove. Percussionists were suddenly in very high demand.

Percussionists are always transporting instruments back and forth between the stage and large drum storage rooms in the bowels of the concert hall. These rooms are filled floor to ceiling with drums of all sizes from everywhere on earth; and also all kinds of bells and whistles, including but not limited to drum sticks and beaters, animal skins, gongs, crash cymbals, tam tams, gongs, trap sets, triangles, chimes, timpani, marimbas, xylophones, tambourines, castanets, wind machines, ratchets, car horns, sirens, washboards, vintage typewriters, and lion's roars. Lastly the room houses lots of tools to keep the stuff in working order. Percussion storage rooms look like a cross between a toy and a hardware store.

For an orchestral percussion audition, this Santa's sleigh of instruments are lined up across the back of the stage in a setup spanning fifteen to twenty feet across. The applicants must bang and crash their way through this musical miniature golf course, demonstrating their proficiency on all the instruments.

Great drummers are shorter than average and more nimble than most folks. Maybe because short people's ears are closer to the earth, they are better positioned to hear and feel the earth's rhythms. Just a thought... Great percussionists are all good drummers. They can make whatever their hands are in contact at a particular moment— a drum kit, triangle, bass drum, xylophone, table top, or car dashboard—*swing*. "It don't mean a thing if it ain't got that swing" is true about all music from Mozart and Bach to Varèse and Louis Armstrong.

Great snare drummers can keep pieces like Ravel's *Daphnis and Chloé* from going off the rails, can place beats 2 and 3 in a Strauss waltz with such perfect *schwung* (swing) that the audience can feel the cork on the champagne bottle pop, or they can lead the entire orchestra and the conductor through a bout of lovemaking, from flirting to fornication, in Ravel's *Bolero*.

A great timpanist can rock a Beethoven or Brahms

symphony just as a great big band drummer can rock a big jazz band. The difference between a timpanist and a big band drummer is that each swings in a different language (and the big band drummer has more fun).

Orchestra percussion sections only get to play when a program includes music written in the last hundred years or so, and they *really* get to play in programs with repertoire from the past fifty. The rest of the time the section sits around, occasionally decorating some loud moments in eighteenth and nineteenth century repertoire.

By far the section's coolest repertoire is written for a percussion ensemble alone—without the rest of the orchestra. Unfortunately, the rest of the orchestra, when enlisted in percussion-centric pieces, does not particularly enjoy playing this "contemporary" repertoire. So while the percussion section is getting busy and having a great time playing pieces by Pierre Boulez, Steve Reich, and Phillip Glass, the rest of the orchestra is grumbling, "This music sure ain't Mozart. Why do I have to waste my time learning this shit?" The grumbling and condescension has very little effect on the percussion section. Not its problem. Percussionists thoroughly enjoy their moments in the spotlight. And when the spotlight is turned off, they can disappear into one of their large storage rooms

and fool around with a recently acquired Nigerian talking drum or put a new head on a bass drum.

Percussionists are always spotted in pairs or groups because they always need each other's help moving stuff around. Percussion is all about team. The musicians function best as a independent unit. To the rest of the orchestra, the percussion section is an exotic foreign destination where the drum tribe resides, happily banging away on all the cool toys. To a drummer, it's home.

Advice for New Drummers

Enjoy your fiefdom! Don't fight with each other; it doesn't matter who plays what part. Rule #1, 2, and 3: Keep the peace back there. Then life in the orchestra will be a breeze.

Harp

A harp glissando is a stairway to something special. It makes people open their eyes a little wider, sit up a little straighter in anticipation of something miraculous about to happen. It is a magic carpet ride (T.V game show host: "You and your bride are going on an all expenses paid vacation to [*cue harp*] ...."). On the other hand, for a split second when people first hear harp music, they think, "Uh oh...Am I being summoned?...Has my card been pulled?" Harpists had been playing "Stairway to Heaven" 5000 years before Led Zeppelin ever leaned in.

The harp is heaven's instrument of choice. The *only* music in heaven is harp music, the perfect musical companion for the afterlife. Composers knew that the sound of the harp evokes in the listener a feeling of being transported to an enchanted realm, an alternate reality. The harp underscores the flawless figurations of the ballet world, the pixilated reflections of sunlight of the French Impressionists in the music of Debussy and Ravel, and the otherworldliness of the fantastical and mythical neighborhoods in opera world (*Lucia di Lammermoor, Die Walkure*).

The harp or lyre was the soundtrack for every balladeer in the ancient world, from Chinese mythical figures, *Fuxi and Shennong*, to Homer, the legendary

Greek storyteller. The harp has even been heard in the outer reaches of our galaxy (see the *Star Trek* episode, "Charlie X," where Uhuru sings while accompanied by Spock on Vulcan harp).

The harp section, like the tuba section, is very small. Usually one person, sometimes two. But unlike the tuba player, who is a part of the brass section, the harp "section" is not part of a larger section. The harp lives in a world all its own. Harp world. "Otherworldly" indeed!

Harpists play in spurts, in parts of pieces, single movements or specific arias. Their services are required only sporadically. To their colleagues, harpists appear to come and go as they please; harpists seem to disappear for weeks on end. Other musicians can only imagine where they go or what they do when they are not playing, but their frequent absence does seem to make the orchestra grow fonder of the sound of the harp when harpists do have occasion to play. There is no one who doesn't enjoy a harp cadenza once in a while or look forward to playing an orchestral solo or singing a song with a harp as a musical partner. The harp allows everyone they play with to relax and play or sing with less force. Playing with a harp is like riding a gentle wave. The harp's transparent tone casts every instrument and voice it accompanies in stark relief; it highlights their sound and brings it into crystal clear focus.

The life of a harpist breaks down into three phases: 1) moving the harp, 2) tuning the harp, and 3) playing the harp. A pedal harp weighs approximately eighty pounds. It has wheels but is too big and unwieldy to take for a ride on a bus or a train and *fuhgeddabout* the subway (not so for a bass violin: I've seen an upright bass lots of times on the subway). A car of adequate size (large hatchback) is required to transport a harp. It lies flat on its side in the back of the car and occupies the same amount of space as four small children. Once the task of moving the harp is completed, the arduous task of tuning it is next.

The harp has forty-seven strings and they all seem to go out of tune every thirty seconds. Harpists are constantly tuning. They probably spend more time tuning the harp than actually playing it.

I have no advice for new harpists. None. The harp is a mystery to me. I am not qualified to give advice. A harpist's job is the most secure job in the orchestra. There is not one instance of a harpist ever being fired from a major symphony orchestra.

Orchestra Piano

There are only a few piano parts in orchestral works, mostly by twentieth and twenty-first century composers. Messiaen, Stravinsky and Bartok made the piano part of the percussion section, to add a tone color to the plucked and struck instruments. Orchestral pianists are thus technically part of the percussion section.... but not exactly... Percussionists have full-time positions but there is not a full-time position for a pianist in the orchestra. Thus, they have very little day to day interaction with members of the orchestra.

Orchestra pianists need to be able follow a conductor. Unfortunately, in their previous experience and training they have seldom had to do this. Even when playing a piano concerto, most pianists don't really follow the conductor; they rely on the conductor to follow them. This often passes for "collaboration," but in my experience real collaboration between conductor and piano soloist happens maybe half the time. (The hallmark of a good conductor is being able to accompany a soloist and make the soloist completely comfortable in their musical interpretation. A bad conductor can never do this.)

When pianists play a piano part in the orchestra,

they must function like any other member of the orchestra and cultivate good 'navigational' skills. They have to follow the conductor and be keenly aware what the other musicians on the stage are playing.

Since every musician plays some piano and there are more people who play piano (or keyboard as it is now often referred to) than any other instrument, there is no particular personality type for an orchestral pianist. But I can say that the orchestra pianist is usually a very lucky person because playing piano in an orchestra is a pretty cushy gig.

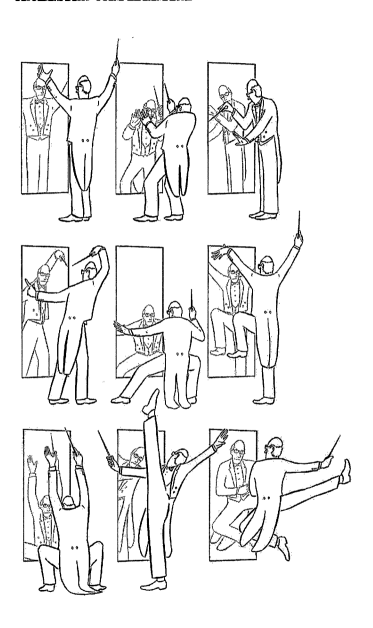

THE CONDUCTOR

"...from God's brain to my heart, I live for art."
—Pink Baby Monster

Music lovers find it difficult to understand what conductors actually do. They see a person waving his or her arms around, carving the air, sculpting phrases with a little stick, and moving various body parts in some sort of rhythm, but often with only a vague relationship to the music coming from the orchestra. They ask, "Would the orchestra play just fine without that guy doing whatever he's doing?..." The answer to this question is YES. But a qualified yes. A good conductor makes each orchestra musician's job easier and the orchestra plays better with a good conductor than with no conductor under most circumstances.

There are many levels of "good" conductors. But all good conductors have three basic attributes:

1) complete knowledge of the music
2) ability to reliably lead the orchestra with clear enough physical gestures
3) ability to stay out of the way just enough to give the musicians enough room to comfortably play their parts.

But performing with no conductor is better than performing with a bad conductor. There are many kinds of bad conductors but they can be broken down into two basic categories: incompetents and posers. Incompetents are either physically inept or musically ignorant. And as you might imagine, incompetents can be both at the same time, spastic and ignorant. Incompetents never have big careers with the symphony or opera but they exist in large numbers in the free-lance music world.

A poser is someone who has a stock portfolio of canned physical gestures that have been rehearsed in front of a mirror. Posers are well known in the world of symphony and opera. They may be competent but their narcissism is distracting and quickly wears thin. Better to play with a robot than a poser.

Ancient Greece produced the first conductor, *Pherekydes of Patrae*, known as the "Giver of Rhythm," around 700 B.C. He reportedly led a group of 800 musicians in what only could be some sort of war chant by beating his golden staff on a resonant box (podium) in a defined rhythm. *He must have been successful, because they won the war.* I'm sure other floor bangers took advantage of this success and followed in their footsteps.

The essence of the job of the conductor has not changed in the 2000 years since. As recently as the late nineteenth century, Richard Wagner summed it up perfectly: "The whole duty of a conductor is comprised in his ability always to indicate the right tempo."

The profundity of this assessment cannot be overstated. The right tempo!

But how a musician conducts has changed. Conductors have graduated from being characterized as just a guy pounding out the rhythm on a wooden box to the lofty status of high priests of classical music, guardians of the Western musical canon. To codify this exalted status, they assumed the title of *maestro*, the term now commonly used for conductor. Moreover, the scope of their duties has changed. They are now the public face of the orchestra, widely assumed by the public to be the interpreter of messages from the musical gods. They are the nexus between the orchestra, board of directors, and the public—the conduit and the consensus builder. It is ironic that the role of oracle of Western classical music falls to a person whose job *makes no sound*.

In order for conductors to be successful, they must first and foremost cultivate a good relationship with the orchestra. Since waving their arms and making expressive faces makes no sound, conductors have no choice but to rely completely on the orchestra to make their "artistic vision" come to life. Good conductors can successfully coordinate the sound of the music (their vision for the way the music should be performed in a specific situation) and how the orchestra interprets the piece. They must effect a consensus. To do so, they must convince the orchestra to respect and trust them, while simultaneously getting the musicians to buy into their musical instincts and ideas so that a harmonious "musical marriage" between the two is made.

Arranging this marriage is more difficult now than in the past because orchestras are now comprised of players who are vastly overqualified. Winning a job in an orchestra is the equivalent of winning the U.S. Open golf tournament, so now orchestras are made up of big winners....stars. Overqualified but, nevertheless, underappreciated. Orchestra players are a fragile lot and must be treated with great delicacy. When a conductor's suggestions or criticisms are not communicated in just the right tone, the orchestra is likely to respond defensively, "How dare you speak to us like that!" They feel disrespected and undervalued.

Autocratic conductors of the past (Toscanini, Szell, Karajan) have disappeared and been replaced by warmer and fuzzier versions. The successful conductor today, almost by necessity, must present him or herself as "person of the people" to be able to "seduce" the overqualified members of the orchestra into believing he or she is really one of them. Many conductors now use social media to reinforce this impression. They post statements like, "the true meaning of music" or "when in the presence of the magisterial greatness of Beethoven, we can only respond with great humility". (If 'drugs' or 'cheeseburgers' were substituted for 'humility', the phrase would make more sense.) These faux-profound utterances may sound great but when unpacked they mean exactly nothing.

This statement like most other social media posts by conductors may come across as disingenuous but at least it shows they are making an effort. But in truth, most conductors pine for the good old days when they had the power of division 1 college football coaches over their "players."

Most conductors do not reach the marriage stage. For the vast majority, the orchestra "swipes left" within the first thirty minutes of the first rehearsal. But for the fortunate few who have the right combination of talent, charm, charisma, and musical intelligence, a wedding takes place.

For guest conductors who work with an orchestra only once a year for a week, absence absolutely makes the heart grow fonder. Such affairs can go on for quite some time.

But in the case of the music director who works with the orchestra all the time, the relationship becomes like a marriage that needs work. Otherwise it begins to deteriorate quite quickly. Marriage can be tricky, especially when only one partner in the marriage has permission to speak.

For the orchestra player, what once was seen as the maestro's brilliant musical insight becomes hackneyed and clichéd over time. The orchestra begins to tire of being told the same things over and over. The little physical gestures that were seen as "cute" during the courtship phase of the relationship become annoying. In rehearsals, the maestro's entreaties and suggestions are likely to be greeted with the blank "perp stares." The fact that the maestro earns ten times what the musicians make and has a dressing room that would be the envy of any rock star, while players have a locker exactly like the one they had in middle school, begins to creep into each musician's thoughts.

Oscar Levant said this sixty years ago and it still

holds true: "A conductor should reconcile himself to the realization that regardless of his approach or temperament the eventual result is the same—the orchestra will hate him."

Surprisingly, the orchestra's feelings toward the conductor have very little relationship to the final product. The music making can be great with a conductor the orchestra dislikes and awful with someone they love. If the conductor is good, the musical results will be good. A case in point is the great maestro, Fritz Reiner, the sadistic music director of the Chicago Symphony Orchestra in the 1950s and 1960s. He was acknowledged by all to be a superb conductor, but when he died the orchestra had a champagne party to celebrate his demise!

The orchestra will not undermine the will of a good conductor they hate because the musicians' artistic integrity prevents them from sabotaging the music. Musicians always want to play well. There are a thousand ways for orchestras to undermine bad conductors, starting with playing how they conducts, following exactly their inept movements, and faithfully reproducing their crappy musical choices and unreliable tempi.

Conductors can have long careers. They routinely conduct well into their 70s and 80s. French horn players are lucky if they play until they're 60.

Conductors have much more room for error than horn players who must form their lips into a specific shape and move a precise amount of air across them in order to play a certain note at specific point in time. Conductors are not bound by these physical limitations. They are free to move six inches this way or that way, jump in the air, drop the baton, etc., all of which has very little effect on the course of the music because the conductor makes no sound. Hence, there is far less pressure on conductors. They don't have to be perfect....Everyone else in the orchestra does!

Advice to Young Conductors

A prerequisite to becoming a successful conductor is love of money and power. It's the conductor's "North Star", the beacon to guide you on your arduous journey through the doldrums and treacherous musical waters, the fuel necessary to reach the podiums of the world's most famous concert halls. If you make it the payoff can be huge.

It has always been better for conductors to say as little as possible and communicate as much as possible through physical gesture. This does not, however, mean flailing around like a person falling off the roof of a ten-story building. Smiling a lot is always good.

The orchestra will probably not pay much attention

to you. Don't feel bad. They're just sizing you up. Simply do your job, don't show off, smile and compliment the orchestra on their wonderful artistry. Lie to them about them being the finest orchestra in the world. (They'll believe it.) Remember that initially your job is to be asked back...Not one person gives a shit about your artistic vision. End rehearsals ten minutes early.

Cultivating an upper-class accent and way of speaking may serve you well with the public and board of directors, but it will not go over very well with the orchestra. A maestro from Brooklyn who tries to sound like a character from Downton Abbey will elicit eye rolls from the orchestra and put you in danger of an immediate "swipe left."

Advice to Old and/or Famous Conductors

Don't forget that it is difficult to distinguish your recording of a standard piece of repertoire from anyone else's recording of the same piece. You are not "special." The 'sound' you get from the orchestra is not much different than the 'sound' the orchestra gets when you are not conducting them.

As you mellow with old age, don't succumb to the temptation to write a book about your life in music. These books are invariably awful pieces of self-aggrandizing boilerplate. They read like the books that politicians write when they are planning a run for high office: bullshit hagiographies of "and then I wrote." These books have self-aggrandizing phases alluding to some kind of sorcery or magic in the titles: 'alchemy of conducting' and the 'mystery behind the baton' etc... A personal memoir will do very little to cement your musical legacy but will confirm some musicians' opinion that you are a pompous ass....who made more money than they did.

Conductors have much more fun than the musicians. The conductor is the driver of the "Rolls Royce", the musicians are the mechanics that make sure the 'car' is in tip-top shape and running smoothly. But now with the arrival of self-driving cars, this may portend a change in this dynamic. The conductor may become obsolete... Just a thought.

Advice for Orchestra Musicians on How to Deal with Conductors

- ✓ Always address a conductor as "maestro." That way you never have to remember a conductor's name. (Avoid using the passive/aggressive, English translation of maestro: "master." This will not work out well for you.)
- ✓ Smile and nod your head in agreement whenever the conductor speaks to you no matter how much you want to say "fuck you."
- ✓ Cultivate a "that was brilliant" look when the conductor speaks to someone in the orchestra. Conductors will notice because they are insecure and always look around for affirmation of their brilliance.
- ✓ Do not ask dumb questions in rehearsal like, "My part says *mezzo forte*, is that what you want?"
- ✓ Remember, you can never win an argument with the conductor. *Conductors make no sound.* You do. This puts you in a no win situation.
- ✓ The conductor is not your enemy; don't take what he says personally.

- ✓ If you play viola and the conductor speaks to you, try not to piss yourself.
- ✓ Do not ask for the conductor's opinion on your playing or the new instrument you are using. The rule is, if you ask, you really don't want to know...
- ✓ Never look guilty when you make a mistake. Make it seem like the other guy screwed up.
- ✓ Never ask the conductor how much money he makes.

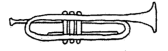

FINAL THOUGHTS

Orchestral musicians are better now than they ever have been in the 400 year-old history of symphony orchestras. Newly minted members of orchestras can boast a level of technical proficiency and training which is better by orders of magnitude than their predecessors. In the United States, there used to be the "top five" orchestras. Now this list could easily be expanded to include twenty five or thirty orchestras given this fact. And if there were enough orchestras to employ all the qualified applicants who seek employment, the list would grow into the hundreds!

This "army" of superlative musicians are as well equipped and outfitted as anyone could hope for to withstand the onslaught of a culture that has not been particularly attentive to the glories of orchestral music. What used to be classical music's core audience, the most highly educated among us, has shifted its attention to more popular musical forms and music from other cultures (world musics). "Classical" music, once the crown jewel of western civilization, has been demoted to "one music among many musics" status. And when the avalanche of information and entertainments: music, movies, videos, snapchats, tweets etc., available at the click of a button are taken into account, the likelihood of leaving home to go to a live concert diminishes. Thus, the task of keeping orchestras alive and well seems quite daunting. Even more, music by dead European white guys becomes a very tough sell in the current cultural climate.

Besides dwindling audiences, there is the question of money for operations. Symphony orchestras are expensive. The operating budget of full time orchestras is around $100 million. And symphony orchestras are not money-making operations. They require the largesse of rich donors to make up the shortfall from ticket sales to enable this musical dinosaur to roam the countryside.

In spite of all these seemingly impossible impediments to performing classical music generally and orchestral music specifically, young musicians from all over the world continue to flock to music schools and conservatories. They do this not because music is a practical or prudent career path but because they LOVE to perform the music. Young classical musicians are intrepid; they are undeterred.

It is my hope that *Orchestra Confidential* will give these wonderfully brave musicians a few moments of levity. It is important to be able to laugh at yourself.

Two things are essential for a life in music:

1) Take the music very seriously.

2) Don't take yourself too seriously.

It is also my hope that *Orchestra Confidential* invites new audiences to have their own peak inside when hearing the glorious sounds of LIVE symphonic music.

About the Author

Mark Gould was co-principal trumpet of the Metropolitan Opera Orchestra from 1974-2003. He has been on the faculty of the Juilliard School since 1982. On 9/11/2001, he founded the performance art group, Pink Baby Monster, which, in 2018, still roams the countryside stirring up trouble.

About the Illustrator

Jeffrey Curnow is a poor, starving illustrator and associate principal trumpet of the Philadelphia Orchestra. His cartoons are published weekly on the NPR Classical Facebook page.